# DAY OF ATONEMENT

A Play in One Act

by
MARGARET WOOD

SAMUEL FRENCH

LONDON

Copyright © 1962 by Margaret Wood
All Rights Reserved

*DAY OF ATONEMENT* is fully protected under the copyright laws of the British Commonwealth, including Canada, the United States of America, and all other countries of the Copyright Union. All rights, including professional and amateur stage productions, recitation, lecturing, public reading, motion picture, radio broadcasting, television and the rights of translation into foreign languages are strictly reserved.

ISBN 978-0-573-02046-9

www.samuelfrench.co.uk
www.samuelfrench.com

---

**FOR AMATEUR PRODUCTION ENQUIRIES**

UNITED KINGDOM AND WORLD
EXCLUDING NORTH AMERICA
plays@SamuelFrench-London.co.uk
020 7255 4302/01

Each title is subject to availability from Samuel French,

depending upon country of performance.

---

CAUTION: Professional and amateur producers are hereby warned that DAY OF ATONEMENT is subject to a licensing fee. Publication of this play does not imply availability for performance. Both amateurs and professionals considering a production are strongly advised to apply to the appropriate agent before starting rehearsals, advertising, or booking a theatre. A licensing fee must be paid whether the title is presented for charity or gain and whether or not admission is charged.

The professional rights in this play are controlled by Samuel French Ltd, 52 Fitzroy Street, London, W1T 5JR.

No one shall make any changes in this title for the purpose of production. No part of this book may be reproduced, stored in a retrieval system, or transmitted in any form, by any means, now known or yet to be invented, including mechanical, electronic, photocopying, recording, videotaping, or otherwise, without the prior written permission of the publisher. No one shall upload this title, or part of this title, to any social media websites.

The right of Margaret Wood to be identified as author of this work has been asserted in accordance with Section 77 of the Copyright, Designs and Patents Act 1988.

For
WILLIAM ASTON

# DAY OF ATONEMENT

*This Play won the British Drama League One Act Play Award and the Geoffrey Whitworth Cup for 1962*

# CHARACTERS

*(in the order of their appearance)*

    JACOB
    MARTHE, his wife
    OTTO, their son
    DR KRAUS, a German

*The action of the Play passes in a room in a displaced persons' camp, somewhere in Germany*

*Time—Late Fifties*

# DAY OF ATONEMENT

Scene—*A room in a displaced persons' camp somewhere in Germany. It is twelve years after the end of hostilities and the relief of the concentration camps.*

*It is a bare comfortless room; there is a door* LC *of the back wall which leads to a passage which in turn leads to the street. There is another door down* L *behind which are clothes-hooks. There is a stove in the corner up* L *on which stands a saucepan of soup and* R *of the stove is a shabby clothes-horse with garments on it. A table stands* RC *with chairs* R, L *and above it; another chair stands against the* L *wall between the door down* L *and the stove. There is a dresser* R *of the* LC *door and against the back wall. On the dresser, apart from a few personal belongings, are three tin plates, three tin mugs, spoons and a loaf of bread. There is a small window in the* R *wall which is covered with shabby curtains. The room is lit by an old-fashioned oil lamp on the table.*

*When the* Curtain *rises,* Jacob, *an elderly Jew, is sitting* L *of the table reading from a Bible. This is held in silence for a few moments; then he slowly closes the book, puts his hand on it and bows his head for a few seconds. Slowly rising, he takes the lamp and the Bible and crosses to the dresser with them. He moves between the dresser and the table, first with a loaf of bread and then with three tin plates and spoons which he places ready for a meal. He moves to the stove and stirs the contents of the saucepan. A door is heard to bang;* Jacob *pauses and listens anxiously.* Marthe, *his wife, enters from the street. They look at each other in silence for a few moments.*

Jacob. Well?
Marthe. She is alive. She has had the operation.
Jacob. When?
Marthe (*taking off her coat*) This morning. I called at the hospital on the way home from work. I did not think they

would let me see her. But Dr Kraus had left word that I could look at her through the glass panel.

JACOB (*taking her coat and hanging it on a peg behind the door*) How is she?

MARTHE (*sitting behind the table; wearily*) Still unconscious. (*With a catch in her voice*) They said to me, "She *is* alive." If they had not told me, I should not have known. She was so white, so still, so peaceful. . . . (*She puts her hand to her quivering mouth*)

JACOB (*putting his arm round her shoulders*) But she *is* alive. Her heart has stood up to it. That's good, Marthe, that's good. It must be very strong, that heart of hers, to stand up to such an operation, you know. She will get well, now.

MARTHE. If only she could. If only she could be really strong and live a normal life, marry, have children . . .

JACOB. Well, now she may. Did you see Dr Kraus?

MARTHE. No, he was out. (*Eagerly*) But he did the operation. He promised Ilse he would. Ilse has such faith in him.

JACOB. Faith means much in such a case.

MARTHE. When they took her away, she said, "It's going to be all right, Momma. Dr Kraus is going to operate himself. Isn't that fine?" She might have been going to a party, she was so gay. I couldn't help crying a little because I thought then that she would never come through that door again. But now she may.

JACOB. No, Marthe, no. She must never come back here, never. The damp and cold of this place gave her tuberculosis. She must go somewhere warmer, drier . . .

MARTHE (*shrugging*) In twelve years we have not found a better place. Is it likely that we shall now?

JACOB (*sitting above the table*) Perhaps Dr Kraus will help us. We'll ask him next time he comes.

MARTHE (*sitting L of the table*) He may come tonight. They told me at the hospital. "Dr Kraus will be round to see you tonight," they said. I thought I might find him here when I got back.

JACOB. Imagine that, now! A busy doctor like Kraus, and he bothers to come to a place like this when his work is done.

MARTHE. Just to bring us a little comfort to face the night with. He is a saint, that man.

JACOB. The cleverest surgeon in the country—and yet he chooses to work among us Jews. That is a wonderful thing for a German to do, you know—after all they've been taught to think of us. Why does he, I wonder?

MARTHE. Because he's a saint—that's what makes saints, —helping the helpless. (*She rises and picks up the bag she put down on entering. She begins to unwrap something inside it, half timidly, half excitedly*) Jacob, I have bought something on the way home. Something for Dr Kraus.

JACOB. What is it?

MARTHE. You won't be angry? It was a little—well—extravagant.

JACOB. When am I angry with you? And when were you last extravagant?

MARTHE (*unwrapping it excitedly*) It's a bottle of wine. We'll drink to Dr Kraus—and to Ilse. (*She puts the bottle on the table*)

JACOB (*picking it up and looking at it*) Wine! When did we last taste wine?

MARTHE (*suddenly still; seeing it all*) On the night they came for us. I remember watching you as you sat with your wine-glass in your hand, listening to the marching feet coming up the street, waiting to see if they would pass our door. (*Shaking her head*) That night they did not pass.

JACOB. And we never finished the wine.

(*Pause*)

MARTHE (*brightening*) But tonight, we will finish it!

JACOB. Yes. And with our enemy who is now our friend. That is right, Marthe, that is how it should be.

MARTHE (*going to the cupboard of the dresser*) No wine-glasses now. Only three tin mugs. Otto will have to have his after Dr Kraus has gone, that's all. (*She brings them back and puts them on the table*)

(JACOB *is easing the cork*)

JACOB. It will warm our hearts, whatever it's in.

(*A door bangs off. They look at each other for a second, uneasily*)

MARTHE. There is Otto, now.

(OTTO *enters from the street. He is young, brooding, a little fanatical. He is dressed in jeans, dark shirt, leather jacket, student's cap*)

OTTO (*anxiously; looking from one to another*) Well?

JACOB. She has had the operation. Your mother has seen her.

OTTO. How is she?

MARTHE. Still unconscious. Very weak, I think, but . . .

OTTO. Weak? Of course she's weak. (*He is taking off his cap and coat as he speaks*) We didn't exactly fatten her up for the occasion, did we?

JACOB. We did our best, my boy.

OTTO. They could have done something at the hospital, couldn't they? To get her stronger first? (*He hangs his coat and cap on the peg of the door down* L)

MARTHE (*crossing to the stove*) But it was urgent, you know it was.

JACOB. After the last haemorrhage they had to work quickly.

OTTO. A pity they didn't work quickly before it.

MARTHE (*doling out the soup*) Don't let's go over all that again. Sit down and have your supper, Otto. You'll feel better then.

(OTTO *sits* R *of the table*)

(*She brings over the soup*) They've done what they could. Dr Kraus operated. He knows what he is doing.

OTTO. *And* what he's done.

JACOB. What does that mean, Otto?

MARTHE. Now, Otto. There's your soup. Eat it and don't argue till you've finished it.

OTTO. That shouldn't take long. (*He begins to drink his soup, sees the wine, pauses, picks it up and reads the label*) Wine? Have we won a lottery or something?

MARTHE. It is for a little celebration. To drink Dr Kraus's health when he comes.

OTTO (*pausing, the spoon half-way to his mouth*) Kraus? Coming here?

MARTHE. Yes. Why?
OTTO. Tonight?
MARTHE. So they told me at the hospital.
OTTO (*rising*) I must go out for a moment.
MARTHE. But, Otto! Your soup! It will get cold.
OTTO. Shan't be long. Put it back on the stove. (*He fetches his jacket and puts it on*)
JACOB (*rising*) Otto. Wait. Where are you going?
OTTO. Only round to Moishe's house.
JACOB. Why now? You passed his house on the way home.
OTTO. I forgot the message then.
JACOB (*going to him*) That's not true. You have just thought of the message. Now. When we said Dr Kraus was coming here.
OTTO (*going to the street door; sullenly*) I'm going.
JACOB (*barring his way*) Otto, Otto. Do you think I don't know my own son? Do you think I don't notice that whenever Kraus is mentioned you become hard and bitter.
MARTHE. After all he has done for us!
JACOB. God forgive me, but there have been times when I thought you would rather have your sister die than let Kraus save her.
OTTO. If what I think of him is true, I would.
MARTHE. Otto! How can you speak such wickedness?
JACOB. What *do* you think of him? Eh? Out with it.
OTTO. I can't yet. I must see Moishe.
JACOB (*with scorn*) To be told what to say? Can't you judge a man by his deeds? Look at his work here in this camp over the last twelve years.
OTTO (*raising his head; vehemently*) And before that? What was he doing before that? Why does he work among throw-outs like us if he's as clever as you say? You two treat him as if he was a saint, or a god. But who is he? Where does he come from?
JACOB. That question might be asked of anyone in this camp. We're all people of nowhere.
OTTO. We, yes. But not the Germans. Where was Kraus in the war?
MARTHE. In the army, I suppose. What are you trying to make us think? What harm has he ever done you?

OTTO. That's what I'm trying to find out.

(OTTO *pushes roughly past Jacob and goes out*)

JACOB (*returning shakily to the table*) Why should he say such things about Kraus?

MARTHE (*almost weeping*) The one man from the outside world who cares about us, and he turns against him.

JACOB (*sitting despondently L of the table*) Put his soup back on the stove, Marthe. He said he would not be long.

(MARTHE *looks at him and does so. Then at his silent brooding figure again*)

MARTHE. What are you thinking about?
JACOB. Otto—and Kraus. They are not pleasant thoughts.
MARTHE. What thoughts?
JACOB. I ask myself the question we asked a few minutes ago. Why should a man of Kraus's talents waste himself with us?
MARTHE (*protesting*) But some people have a vocation for such work. Look at Vincent de Paul—look at Schweizer, look . . .
JACOB. What was he doing in the war? When we were in the concentration camps, where was Kraus?
MARTHE. Why, in the army. You cannot blame a man for being in his country's army.
JACOB. I am blaming no-one. I am trying to understand.
MARTHE. What?
JACOB. What Otto has found out.

(*A door bangs off; there is a pause, then a knock*)

JACOB (*in a whisper*) Kraus!
MARTHE. Bringing us news of Ilse. Remember that. Don't think of Otto now. Think of Ilse. (*She goes to the street door and opens it*)

(KRAUS *stands outside. He is tired*)

KRAUS. Ah, good. I was afraid, for a moment, that you weren't in.
MARTHE. Oh, come in, Doctor, come in. It is good of you

# DAY OF ATONEMENT

to come when you are so tired. How is she?

KRAUS (*patting her kindly on the shoulder*) It's all right, Marthe. She's going to pull through. Her heart stood up to it better than I expected.

(MARTHE *goes quickly to Jacob and hugs him*)

She's brave your daughter. She's a fighter and that's half the battle.

MARTHE. And you're the other half, Doctor. Without you she would have been dead by now—oh, it's true.

(KRAUS *protests*)

She will get better because you are in charge. Without you . . . (*She shrugs*)

KRAUS. Well, I just came to tell you that everything's satisfactory. I mustn't interrupt your supper.

MARTHE. No. No. Please don't go yet. Sit down, please sit down—we've something special—for you!

KRAUS. Me? (*He sits behind the table laughing*)

(MARTHE *moves* R *of the table*. JACOB *is* L *of it*)

JACOB (*holding up the bottle; proudly*) Wine!

KRAUS. Wine! Oh, but you shouldn't . . .

MARTHE. Oh, yes. Just for this once. While Ilse is in hospital, you see, we do not need to spend much on food. So we can afford wine for such a special occasion—and for such a special friend.

JACOB. And now we have something to drink to. It is a long time since we could say that. First we drink to you! Dr Kraus, your health!

(MARTHE *and* JACOB *stand while they drink*. KRAUS *remains seated*)

MARTHE. And our love and thanks.

KRAUS (*moved*) Thank you, Marthe, thank you, Jacob. You don't know how much it means to me, to have your gratitude. And now (*He rises*) let's drink to Ilse, and a happy, healthy future for her.

MARTHE }
JACOB  } (*together*) To Ilse!

JACOB. And a happy healthy future!

KRAUS (*sitting*) It's about the future that I want to talk to you. Ilse must not come back here.

MARTHE (*sitting R of the table*) That is the very thing that we wanted to ask you about.

JACOB (*turning away* C) We're ashamed to ask for help when you have already done so much, but where can we turn?—You know, Doctor, I was once the head of a big business, I had many men under me—but now... (*He shrugs*) I do not know any longer how one makes arrangements for anything. We have been out of the world too long.

MARTHE. And then there's the money. We have only just enough with what I earn from my cleaning jobs, and what Otto brings home from the garage. Jacob sometimes earns a little, clearing the rubble from the bombed sites.

KRAUS (*sharply*) I have told you before, Jacob, that your heart can't stand such work.

JACOB (*with spirit*) What else is there for a man of my age? The heart can die in more ways than one.

KRAUS. All right, Jacob, all right. Let's get back to Ilse. For six weeks, I can get her into a sanatorium. After that, she must go elsewhere. Somewhere warm, if possible.

MARTHE. If only she could go home—to Israel.

KRAUS (*surprised*) I didn't know you'd ever been in Palestine.

MARTHE. Oh, we haven't. But Israel is the home of every Jew, whether he has been there or not.

JACOB. You know, Dr Kraus, at every Passover we have a special meal to remind us of the time when Moses led the children of Israel out of the land of bondage. They ate that last meal secretly, in haste, ready to escape to the Promised Land.

KRAUS. So I have heard.

JACOB. And at the end of that meal we always stand—wherever we are in the world, (*he picks up his mug*) and we raise our glasses and say, "To next year, in Jerusalem!"

MARTHE (*fervently, raising her mug*) To next year, in Jerusalem!

(*They both drink*)

KRAUS. You say this? Always?
JACOB. Always. (*He sits* L *of the table*) All through the centuries, our people have never lost sight of the vision of the home they have never seen. (*With a deprecating laugh*) But for centuries it has been just a bit of ritual, you know. We said it, but we could never really believe it would happen. Israel didn't exist. We had no home.
MARTHE. But now it is real. The Jews have a home again. Otto and Ilse must go to Israel.
KRAUS. And you?
JACOB (*sadly*) No. We have had to wait too long. We shan't see the Promised Land.
KRAUS (*moved; rising*) I will see what I can do. There are organizations—funds—you must all go.
MARTHE. It is enough if the children go.
KRAUS. No, it must be the family. If necessary I will pay for Otto and Ilse myself.
MARTHE (*rising*) Oh, no, Doctor. You've already done so much . . .
KRAUS (*moving* L) It must be the family, I tell you. Ilse needs her mother and father. And Otto does, too. In fact it's as urgent to get him away from here as it is for Ilse.

(JACOB *and* MARTHE *look at each other*)

MARTHE (*going to him*) You mean he is going with bad boys—with a gang.
KRAUS. Yes. He would be better away, I think.
MARTHE. I know, I know. (*Pleading*) But he is a good boy, really, Doctor, a good boy. He gives us nearly all his wages.
JACOB. But inside he is turning hard, bitter—suspicious.
KRAUS. Of whom?
JACOB (*evasively*) Of people who have helped us.
KRAUS. Of me? Well? Go on. It's me he's suspicious of, isn't it?
JACOB (*unwillingly*) Yes, of you.

(*The door opens and shuts, off* C)

KRAUS. Why?
JACOB. How should we know?

(OTTO *enters* C, *stops short on seeing Kraus and then turns and goes out*)

MARTHE (*going to the door and calling*) Otto! Otto! Didn't you see Dr Kraus? He's come to tell us about Ilse . . .
OTTO (*off*) One moment. I am coming back.
MARTHE (*looking off*) He's talking to someone outside.

(*The door bangs and* OTTO *returns*)

Who was that at the door?
OTTO (*brushing past her*) Friends. I told them to wait. (*He keeps his eyes fixed on Kraus*)
MARTHE. Why? Are you going out again?
OTTO (*still looking at Kraus*) Possibly.
JACOB (*rising; sharply*) Otto! That's no way to speak to your mother.
OTTO. I'm sorry, Mother.
JACOB. And no way to treat a guest and benefactor. You have not yet greeted Dr Kraus.
OTTO (*going up to him*) Kraus? Kraus? Are you *sure* this is Dr Kraus?
MARTHE. Otto! Please. Dr Kraus, don't think he's always like . . .
JACOB. You will explain your behaviour immediately, Otto.
OTTO. Immediately. Mother wait in the next room. This is a man's business.
MARTHE (*looking quickly from one to the other*) No. Man's business is cruel business as often as not. Moreover, you are not a man, but a boy. A very naughty boy. So, I stay. (*She sits, firmly* R *of the table*)
OTTO. Please, Mother.
MARTHE. I stay!
OTTO (*shrugging*) Very well.
JACOB. Otto, if you had been here five minutes ago, you would have heard what Dr Kraus offered to do for you and Ilse.
OTTO. Whatever he offered, I should refuse it.
JACOB (*thumping his hand on the table*) Silence! He offered to pay for you and Ilse to go to Israel.
OTTO. Kraus offered this?

JACOB. *Dr* Kraus offered it.
OTTO. Why?
MARTHE. Why? Why? Because he is a good man. He has saved Ilse, and now he wants to save you.
OTTO. Ilse perhaps. But why me? (*He advances right up to Kraus*) Why me?
KRAUS (*steadily*) Because I want to keep the family together: your sister needs you: your parents need you: and you most certainly need your parents.
OTTO. Are you sure it isn't because you're anxious to get me away from here?
KRAUS. Why should I do that?
OTTO. Because I know too much.
KRAUS (*turning away down* L; *with an attempt at lightness*) I should have thought the reverse. You have much to learn.
OTTO. I can tell you one thing I have learnt, Dr Kraus.
KRAUS. Well?
OTTO. That your name is not Kraus, but Holtz.

(KRAUS *stiffens slightly and becomes very still, looking out front*)

MARTHE. Nonsense!
OTTO. Holtz. That was his name when he was doctor of a concentration camp.

(*There is an appalled silence*)

JACOB (*sitting* L *of the table, shakily; in a whisper*) Concentration camp?
MARTHE (*rising*) It's not true! He's a good man. Jacob say something!
OTTO (*behind Jacob's chair*) Yes, Father. What have you to say?
JACOB (*quietly*) I am waiting for Dr Kraus to speak.
KRAUS. And I am waiting for Otto's proof.
OTTO. Moishe's father recognized him.
MARTHE (*scornfully*) Moishe's father! They have only just come here.
OTTO. Which is why he has not been recognized before.
MARTHE. Moishe's father, indeed! What does he know of Dr Kraus's work for us here in this camp?

OTTO. Very little. But they know of his work in those other camps.

JACOB. What work?

OTTO (*advancing on Kraus*) Surgery on the healthy; operations to mutilate the strong; experiments to see how much the human body can stand without actually dying...

MARTHE (*crying out*) No! It can't be true, it can't be!

OTTO. Let him deny it, then. Go on. Deny that you've done these things; deny that you've watched hundreds go into the gas chambers, and checked through the piles of bodies at the end of it. Deny...

MARTHE (*in tears*) You are wicked, Otto. Wicked to say such terrible, terrible things.

JACOB. Dr Kraus. What do you say?

KRAUS. I am still waiting for Otto's proof.

OTTO (*suddenly gripping his arm*) Then take that glove off your right hand.

KRAUS. I have a skin disease. It's a great affliction for a surgeon. Besides, it's unpleasant to look at. Why should I take it off?

OTTO. Why shouldn't you if a skin disease is all that troubles you? We're not squeamish.

KRAUS. And if I refuse?

OTTO. You will not refuse. (*He produces a revolver*)

MARTHE (*crying out*) Otto!

JACOB (*rising*) Otto, you know I will not have weapons in this house.

OTTO. I'm sorry, Father. You have no choice.

JACOB. You dare to tell me that I have no...

OTTO (*overriding him*) If Kraus has no scar on his hand I promise I will apologize and give you the gun at once.

MARTHE. What scar?

OTTO (*circling above Kraus and coming down* L, *keeping him covered*) The mark of a swastika, branded on to the palm of his hand by Jewish prisoners on the day of liberation. *That is his skin affection.*

MARTHE (*running to Kraus and clinging to his hand*) No, no. It's not true. It can't be true. Don't take it off. (*Weeping*) Let me believe there is nothing.

OTTO. You'd never really believe it, Mother. You'd be

tortured by doubts for the rest of your life. Come on, Kraus. Prove your innocence.

(*A pause. They are all watching Kraus.* KRAUS *is looking at Otto*)

KRAUS (*quietly*) Be merciful, Otto. Shoot me now, quickly.

(OTTO *gives a long sigh.* JACOB *slowly covers his face with his hand, and sits, shakily.* MARTHE *is still too stunned to take it in*)

OTTO. Shooting's too good for you. You'll stand your trial as a war criminal.

MARTHE (*dazed*) Shoot? What are you saying?

(KRAUS *holds out to her the hand from which he has peeled the glove.* MARTHE *looks at it and turns away, her clenched hands to her mouth.* KRAUS *crosses to Jacob and holds it out, but* JACOB *gestures it away without looking*)

OTTO (*triumphantly*) Well, Father?

JACOB (*muttering*) Nothing in haste—nothing in haste. We must think.

OTTO. Yes, think, Father. It shouldn't be difficult to remember the six million Jews who died in Germany.

JACOB. I remember them every day of my life. But at this moment I am thinking of Dr Kraus. (*To him*) I can't understand . . . Why did you stay in Europe? Why come to a camp like this where you might be recognized, as Moishe's father has recognized you?

KRAUS. I had a debt to pay.

JACOB. To whom?

KRAUS. To you. The Jewish people.

OTTO. You expect us to swallow that? Don't believe him, Father. He's just trying to soft-soap his way out of it.

JACOB (*rising*) But I do believe it. If he could take another name and come here, he could have taken another name and got away—to another country. *We* know how he has worked these last twelve years . . .

OTTO. That doesn't excuse what he has done. Mother, what do you say?

(MARTHE *crosses to the dresser and turns her back*)

MARTHE. I don't know—I can't think. I only know that whatever he's done in the past, he has saved Ilse now. (*Turning to Kraus*) How could you, *could* you do such things? (*She sits* R *of the table, weeping*)

(KRAUS *remains standing, with* OTTO *covering him*)

KRAUS. At first it was hard. Then it became—less hard. In the end, I did not feel anything at all. The longer one lives with evil, the less one thinks of good.

JACOB. That is true, very true ... (*He turns away up stage, by the dresser*)

KRAUS. I came back to try to save some of the people I had helped to destroy. For twelve years I have tried to atone a little.

OTTO (*contemptuously*) Atone!

KRAUS. I didn't think I should have so long—but I'm glad the end has come.

JACOB. Has the end come?

KRAUS. Oh, yes. If Otto doesn't shoot me, the court will hang me.

OTTO. That's true. Moishe and his father are waiting to hand him over.

MARTHE. No. There's another way out—through that door and up to the roof ... (*She starts forward towards the door* L)

OTTO. Mother, I'm warning you. If he moves from this room except by my orders, I shall shoot. But I don't want to. Let him stand his trial and hang.

JACOB (*turning and coming down* R *of Kraus*) What good will that do? What difference does it make to our six million dead that twelve years after, you kill the man who helped to kill them?

OTTO. What would *you* do, then?

JACOB. Let him go, perhaps?

OTTO (*outraged*) Let him go? Are you crazy? Do you think we can just forget all he's done?

JACOB. Not forget. I can never forget—or forgive.

OTTO. Of course you can't.

JACOB. But neither will I take revenge.
OTTO. You must! Any good Jew wants to avenge his dead!
JACOB. Nine out of ten, perhaps. I hope to be the tenth.
OTTO. Then you're a coward!
MARTHE. You know that's a lie.
JACOB (*wearily*) What have cowardice or courage got to do with it? To avenge in hot blood is one thing; to avenge in blood that has been cooling twelve years is another.
OTTO. Mine has not cooled.
MARTHE (*wringing her hands*) I still can't believe it . . . (*To Kraus*) You, who are so kind and generous. How could you stand by and see such things done?
OTTO (*harshly*) He didn't just stand by. He did them.
KRAUS (*sharply*) I had my orders. I had to carry them out. If I hadn't, I should have suffered the same fate.
OTTO. Why not suffer it?
KRAUS. I ask myself that now. But then there seemed much to live for—my young wife—my two babies. They would have suffered too—but in the end . . . (*He hesitates*)
JACOB. Well?
KRAUS. I need not have troubled. They were killed when the British bombed Berlin.
JACOB (*shaking his head*) Aie, aie. No-one is righteous in war. We are all evil.
KRAUS. After that, I did my beastly work with a better heart, as if the Jews were responsible, poor devils.
OTTO. That's enough. By God it's enough. Get moving, Holtz.

(KRAUS *moves to the* C *door, but* JACOB *blocks the way*)

JACOB. Not yet.
OTTO. Yes, Father. We've argued long enough. Moishe and his father are waiting.
JACOB. Let them wait. You spoke of justice, Otto. I spoke of mercy. If he goes through this door he will get neither.
OTTO. Did *he* show either justice or mercy?
JACOB. That is not the point. Has he atoned? That is

what God would ask. So we will ask it too. Sit down, Dr Kraus.

(DR KRAUS *sits* L *of the table*)

And, Otto, you will sit also.

(*There is a battle of wills. Then* OTTO *sits, sulkily, by the door down* L*., keeping Kraus covered all the time*)

You say that you were much more bitter towards us after the deaths of your wife and children. Yet you have risked your life for twelve years to work among us. What made you change?

KRAUS. A Jew. His name was Baecke.
MARTHE. Carl Baecke? Of the Theresienstadt camp?
KRAUS. Yes.
JACOB. A great man. A fine rabbi. What happened?
KRAUS. I think it began when I was told that he was holding meetings in one of the huts after lights out. His wife and four sisters had already died in another camp; he expected death at any moment. So we thought that he might be planning a revolt. He had nothing to lose. One night I slipped quietly into the back of the hut.
MARTHE. Yes? (*She sits* R *of the table, keeping her eyes on Kraus all the time*)
KRAUS (*moved*) I shall never forget what I saw. The place was crammed with those poor starved scarecrows. They sat or lay on the floor, they hung in clusters to the tiers of bunks. Carl Baecke was the only one who saw me enter. He bowed to me slightly, for all the world as if I were a student apologizing for coming in late—and went on talking.
OTTO. What about? A plot?
KRAUS. No. About Plato.
OTTO (*incredulous*) Plato?
JACOB. What did you do?
KRAUS. Nothing. That winter he gave a course of lectures on the history of philosophy, from Plato to Kant. He did not always have the same audience. Many who listened one night were dead the next, but others took their places.

MARTHE. But you let him lecture to them. That was something.
KRAUS. Not enough. (*He rises and moves down* R)

(OTTO *also rises keeping Kraus covered*)

But it was then that I began to ask myself questions. You see, we had been told that the Jews were the scum of the earth until we believed it. (*He moves* R *of the table to the up* R *corner as he speaks*) Oh, I know that we ought not to have done, but we did. Yet here was a rabbi, speaking night after night to these condemned skeletons as if he were in a university—and about philosophy! In my heart I knew that this was a great man and that these were great people.

OTTO (*harshly*) But you still let them go to the gas chambers.

(KRAUS *bows his head and opens his hands in a helpless gesture of acknowledgement*)

MARTHE. And then?
KRAUS. Then suddenly the war was over. For the last few weeks we had had little news, and always contradictory. Then one day, the Russians were in the camp. The Russian commander had no time to bother with us. They were pressing westward. So he—he handed us over to our own prisoners. (*He wipes the sweat off his forehead*) I shall never forget the sardonic grin on his face as he left us in the middle of that mob.

JACOB. I have heard the end of this story. It has spread through all the Jews left in Europe. But tell Otto. It may teach him something.

KRAUS (*looking at his hand*) They had already put this mark on me and they were going to—(*he blinks at the memory*) do other things, when Carl Baecke found us. He stopped them. He stood between us and that raging crowd and forbade them to touch us. And they obeyed! One man against hundreds. After all we had done to them—and they obeyed! He kept us safe until the authorities arrived and then handed us over. But there was still much confusion, and I managed to escape.

JACOB (*softly*) But you didn't leave Europe.

KRAUS. No. At first I thought I would try. But then I thought of Baecke. He'd saved me for something more than that. So I came here to work till I should be discovered. It has been a long time. I'm ready to go, Otto.

(OTTO *and* KRAUS *move to the door* C)

MARTHE (*rising and interposing between them*) Not that way. He has earned the way through the other door. Go, quickly, Dr Kraus—up to the attic and over the roofs ...

OTTO (*moving in front of the door down* L) Move one step to this door and I shall shoot.

MARTHE (*turning on him*) Otto, you are a silly boy. You understand nothing because you have suffered nothing. No! You will not speak. You have all talked, you three men, and I have listened. Now I will have my say. Jacob, you are right. He has atoned. We must stop hating and try to forgive.

OTTO. I will never forgive.

MARTHE (*sharply*) Leave forgiveness to those who have something to forgive. Dr Kraus, you spoke of Carl Baecke. I ask myself now what he would have done if he were here.

OTTO. He's not here and I am: and I have the gun.

MARTHE (*quieter*) There is goodness in you, Otto; I know that you can be gentle and loving: but now you are full of hate, and the more you live with hate the more evil you will become. Hatred turns inward, and multiplies like a cancer; love turns outward to others. No-one knows that better than Dr Kraus. He has lived with both.

JACOB. That's well said, Marthe.

OTTO. Mother, I've no time to argue any more. Get out of the way.

MARTHE. I will not. If you want to shoot Dr Kraus, you will have to shoot me first.

JACOB (*anxiously*) Marthe!

OTTO. I'm warning you, Mother!

MARTHE. Otto, Otto! Any child or madman with a gun thinks himself a fine strong hero when the other man has none. But he is still only a child or a madman. And when he has shot and killed he does not know how to use the power that is his. (*With growing vehemence*) And so it goes on and on. You killed because he killed; and someone will kill you because you killed him. Violence and hatred: hatred and violence. Round and round they go for ever and ever, because no-one has the courage to break the circle. But *this time*, this time it *shall* be broken. We will not revenge. We will forgive.

OTTO. Never!

MARTHE (*sweeping on*) Sometime, somewhere, someone must stop and say, "This shall go no further! We will forgive!"

OTTO. Woman's talk, woman's talk! They'd say we were cowards.

MARTHE. I will show you how much of a coward I am! (*She suddenly walks straight up to Otto, taking him by surprise, and seizing the muzzle of the revolver, holds it against her breast*)

OTTO (*startled and scared*) Mother! Take care! It's cocked!

MARTHE. So—it's cocked. Good. A very little struggle will set it off. Dr Kraus, quickly, now, before the other people in the house get in.

OTTO (*shouting*) Mother, for God's sake, let go.

MARTHE. For God's sake I hold on!

JACOB ⎱ (*together*) ⎧ Let her have it, Otto. Don't struggle.
KRAUS ⎰ ⎩ Stop! Stop, both of you!

(OTTO, *in terror and despair, lets go of the gun.* MARTHE *looks at it for a moment, then crosses to the dresser and puts it in a drawer*)

OTTO (*sobbing with fright and anger*) You've tricked me! You're traitors, both of you, and everyone'll know it. They'll all know you let him go . . .

KRAUS. It's all right, Otto. I'm not going. I'm coming with you.

MARTHE. No!

KRAUS. Yes, Marthe. Believe me, it's better so. I would not make bad blood in this family for all the freedom in the world. I'll stand my trial.

MARTHE (*tonelessly*) They will hang you.

KRAUS. Yes.

MARTHE. After they have opened all the old wounds again, they will hang you.
KRAUS. I know.
MARTHE. What's the *good* of it all? They will go over it again and again, and each time it will breed more hate and more evil. Why can't we remember the goodness of people instead of the wickedness?
JACOB. That much we can do for him, Marthe. We can speak for him at his trial. We can tell them what he has done for us here all these years, and what he has done for Ilse.
MARTHE (*realizing her full loss*) Ilse, my poor Ilse! This will kill her.
KRAUS. No, Marthe. She is in good hands. She need know nothing till she is stronger. Let us go, Otto.
JACOB. I will not have my son play any further part in this. He will stay here.
OTTO. It would be better if you let me go.
JACOB. I am still master in my own house. You will stay.
OTTO. I'm warning you . . .
JACOB. You will stay!
OTTO (*sullenly*) Very well. Moishe and his father are waiting.
KRAUS. Good-bye, Marthe. Good-bye, Jacob. Tell Ilse I'm relying on her to get really strong.

(KRAUS *goes out* C. MARTHE *weeps on Jacob's shoulder.* OTTO *moves swiftly to the door and watches him go*)

JACOB. The Lord bless him and keep him. The Lord make His face to shine upon him and be gracious unto him.

(*The door bangs. Almost immediately there is a volley of shots.* MARTHE *raises her head, startled.* OTTO *stiffens*)

(*Softly*) The Lord lift up the light of His countenance upon him and give him peace.
MARTHE. What was that? What have they done to him? (*She starts towards the door* C)
OTTO (*holding her*) Don't go, Mother, please don't go.
MARTHE (*gripping Otto by the front of his jacket*) What have you done? They've killed him and you knew they would.

You knew! You knew! (*She is sobbing and shaking him in her despair*)

OTTO (*half hysterical*) It's your fault! If you'd let me go with him, they wouldn't have shot him. I knew you might stop me—or he might have a gun—so we arranged. If I brought him out, we'd just arrest him and make him stand trial. If he came alone, it meant trouble, and they were to shoot. *You* sent him out alone. *You* stopped me going. It's your fault, it's your fault . . .

(MARTHE *releases* OTTO *and he drops sobbing into the chair by the door* L. MARTHE, *shattered, goes to* JACOB)

JACOB (*putting his arm around Marthe*) When shall we learn, O Lord, when shall we learn to forsake evil and do good? Don't cry, Marthe. God will be more merciful to him than we have been. Otto, stand up.

(OTTO *stands, gulping and wiping his eyes with the back of his hand, suddenly young and vulnerable*)

Now we must learn to forgive each other. Bring me the Book.

(OTTO *turns to the dresser and brings the Bible to the table*)

Open it at the Psalms of David, the one hundred and thirtieth . . .

(OTTO *finds it, and proffers it to Jacob*)

JACOB. No. You will read it.
OTTO. I—can't.
JACOB. Read it. It will help you.
OTTO (*stumblingly*)
Out of the deep have I called to thee, O Lord.
Lord, hear my voice and consider well my supplication.
If thou, O Lord, should call our sins to account
Who could stand against thee?
But there is mercy in thee; therefore—therefore . . .
(*He breaks down*)
JACOB (*taking it up strongly*)
My soul longs for the Lord, even more than the watchmen
    for the morning.

O Israel, trust in the Lord, for in Him there is steadfast love.
(*He stretches out his hand and draws Otto to him*)
And He will redeem us from all our iniquities.

**CURTAIN**

# FURNITURE AND PROPERTY LIST

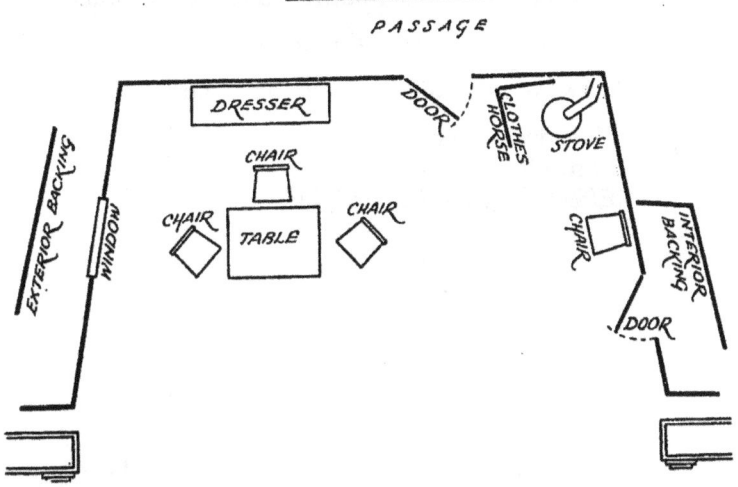

*On stage:* Table. *On it:* old-fashioned oil lamp, Bible
            4 upright chairs
            Dresser. *On it:* loaf of bread, 3 tin plates, 3 tin mugs, spoons
            Stove. *On it:* saucepan of soup
            Clothes-horse. *On it:* garments
            Shabby curtains at window
            Clothes-hooks behind the door down L

*Off stage:* Shopping bag. *In it:* bottle of wine (wrapped) (MARTHE)

*Personal:* KRAUS: handkerchief, a glove for his right hand
           OTTO: revolver

# LIGHTING PLOT

Property fittings required: old-fashioned oil lamp (practical)

Interior. The same scene throughout

THE MAIN ACTING AREAS are RC, up C, LC

*To open:* Curtains drawn
Lamp lit
Effect of general lamplight

*No cues*

# EFFECTS PLOT

| | | |
|---|---|---|
| Cue 1 | JACOB stirs saucepan<br>*Door bang* | (Page 1) |
| Cue 2 | JACOB: ". . . whatever it's in."<br>*Door bang* | (Page 3) |
| Cue 3 | JACOB: ". . . has found out."<br>*Door bang followed, after a pause, by a knock* | (Page 6) |
| Cue 4 | JACOB: "Yes, of you."<br>*Sound of door opening and shutting* | (Page 9) |
| Cue 5 | MARTHE: ". . . to someone outside."<br>*Door bang* | (Page 10) |
| Cue 6 | JACOB: ". . . gracious unto him."<br>*Door bang followed by a volley of shots* | (Page 20) |

www.ingramcontent.com/pod-product-compliance
Lightning Source LLC
Chambersburg PA
CBHW070455050426
42450CB00012B/3282